WINTER WARMERS

Baking

igloobooks

Published in 2016
by Igloo Books Ltd
Cottage Farm
Sywell
NN6 0BJ
www.igloobooks.com

Food photography and recipe development
© Stockfood, The Food Media Agency

Cover image: © iStock / Getty

Cover designed by Nicholas Gage
Edited by Natalie Baker

LEO002 0916
2 4 6 8 10 9 7 5 3 1
ISBN 978-1-78670-149-7

Printed and manufactured in China

CONTENTS

BAKERS' CLASSICS

CHEESE AND BACON SCONES

MAKES
12

PREPARATION TIME: 15 MINUTES
COOKING TIME: 15 MINUTES

1 tbsp olive oil

3 rashers streaky bacon, finely chopped

75 g / 2 ½ oz / ⅓ cup butter, cubed

150 g / 5 ½ oz / 1 cup self-raising flour, plus extra for dusting

100 g / 3 ½ oz / ⅔ cup wholemeal flour

½ tsp mustard powder

¼ tsp Cayenne pepper

3 spring onions (scallions), chopped

150 ml / 5 ½ fl. oz. / ⅔ cup milk, plus extra for brushing

100 g / 3 ½ oz / 1 cup Red Leicester cheese, grated

METHOD

- Preheat the oven to 220°C (200°C fan) / 425F / gas 7 and line two baking trays with greaseproof paper.

- Heat the oil in a frying pan and fry the bacon for 2 minutes or until golden brown. Leave to cool.

- Rub the butter into the two flours and then stir in the mustard powder, Cayenne pepper, spring onions and bacon. Add the milk and ¾ of the cheese and mix together into a soft dough, adding a little more milk if necessary.

- Divide the dough into 12 equal pieces and shape into rough rounds, then spread them out on the baking trays. Brush the scones with milk, sprinkle with the rest of the cheese and bake for 15 minutes or until golden brown and cooked through.

- Transfer the scones to a wire rack to cool a little before serving.

WHITE COUNTRY LOAVES

MAKES
2

PREPARATION TIME: 3 HOURS
COOKING TIME: 40 MINUTES

800 g / 1 lb 12 oz / 5 ⅓ cups strong white bread flour

1 tsp easy blend dried yeast

2 tbsp caster (superfine) sugar

2 tsp fine sea salt

2 tbsp butter, melted

METHOD

- Mix together the flour, yeast, sugar and salt. Stir the butter into 560 ml of warm water then stir it into the dry ingredients.

- Knead the mixture on a lightly oiled surface for 10 minutes or until smooth and elastic. Leave the dough to rest in an oiled bowl, covered with oiled cling film, for 1–2 hours or until doubled in size.

- Knead for 2 minutes then divide into two. Shape into round loaves and transfer to two oiled baking trays. Cover with oiled cling film and leave to prove for 1 hour or until doubled in size.

- Meanwhile, preheat the oven to 220°C (200°C fan) / 425F / gas 7.

- Make decorative slashes in the top of the loaves with a sharp knife or scalpel then bake for 40 minutes or until they sound hollow when you tap them underneath. Transfer to a wire rack and leave to cool completely before cutting.

LEEK AND PARMESAN CHOUX BUNS

MAKES
16

PREPARATION TIME: 20 MINUTES
COOKING TIME: 25 MINUTES

1 small leek, trimmed and chopped

2 tbsp olive oil

55 g / 2 oz / ¼ cup butter, cubed

75 g / 2 ½ oz / ½ cup strong white bread flour, sieved

2 large eggs, beaten

50 g / 1 ¾ oz / ½ cup Parmesan, finely grated

METHOD

• Preheat the oven to 200°C (180°C fan) / 400F / gas 6.

• Fry the leeks in the oil for 6 minutes to soften.

• Oil and line a large baking tray with greaseproof paper, then spray it with a little water.

• Put the butter in a saucepan with 150 ml water and heat until the butter melts and the water starts to boil.

• Turn off the heat and immediately beat in the flour with a wooden spoon until it forms a smooth ball of pastry.

• Stir in the egg a little at a time until you have a glossy paste then beat in the Parmesan and leeks.

• Spoon the pastry into a piping bag fitted with a large star nozzle and pipe 2.5 cm (1 in) buns onto the baking tray.

• Bake for 10 minutes, then increase the heat to 220°C (200°C fan) / 425F / gas 7 and bake for another 10 minutes.

• Transfer the choux buns to a wire rack and make a small hole in the underneath of each one with a skewer so the steam can escape.

DUTCH EASTER BUNNY BREAD

MAKES
6

PREPARATION TIME: 3 HOURS 30 MINUTES
COOKING TIME: 15 MINUTES

400 g / 14 oz / 2 ⅔ cups strong white bread flour

½ tsp easy blend dried yeast

4 tbsp caster (superfine) sugar

1 tsp fine sea salt

50 g / 1 ¾ oz / ¼ cup butter, melted

1 tsp vanilla extract

250 ml / 9 fl. oz / 1 cup milk, warmed

6 quails' eggs

12 raisins

METHOD

- Mix together the flour, yeast, sugar and salt. Stir the butter and vanilla into the milk then stir it into the dry ingredients. Knead the mixture on a lightly oiled surface with your hands for 10 minutes or until the dough is smooth and elastic.

- Leave it to rest in a lightly greased bowl, covered with greased cling film, for 2 hours or until doubled in size.

- Knead the dough for 2 minutes, then divide it into six pieces and roll each one into a rectangle. Cut the top third of each rectangle into four strands. The middle two strands will form the ears. Press a quails' egg into the centre of each 'bunny' and pull the outer two strands down and over the egg as if the bunny is holding it. Pinch together to seal, then add two raisin eyes to each one.

- Spread them out on a greased baking tray then cover with oiled cling film and leave to prove for 1 hour or until doubled in size.

- Preheat the oven to 220°C (200°C fan) / 425F / gas 7. Bake the bunnies for 15 minutes or until the bases sound hollow when tapped. Transfer to a wire rack and leave to cool before serving.

CHEESE SCONES

MAKES
12

PREPARATION TIME: 10 MINUTES
COOKING TIME: 12 – 15 MINUTES

75 g / 2 ½ oz / ⅓ cup butter, cubed

250 g / 9 oz / 1 ⅔ cups self-raising flour, plus extra for dusting

½ tsp mustard powder

¼ tsp Cayenne pepper

150 ml / 5 ½ fl. oz / ⅔ cup milk, plus extra for brushing

100 g / 3 ½ oz / 1 cup Red Leicester cheese, grated

METHOD

• Preheat the oven to 220°C (200°C fan) / 425F / gas 7 and line a baking tray with greaseproof paper.

• Rub the butter into the flour with your fingertips until the mixture resembles fine breadcrumbs then stir in the mustard powder and Cayenne pepper.

• Add the milk and ¾ of the cheese and mix together into a pliable dough.

• Turn the dough out onto a floured work surface and flatten it into a rectangle, 2 cm (1 in) thick.

• Use a round pastry cutter to stamp out the scones then transfer them to the baking tray.

• Brush the scones with milk, sprinkle with the rest of the cheese and bake for 12–15 minutes or until golden brown and cooked through.

• Transfer the scones to a wire rack to cool a little before serving.

WHOLEMEAL SESAME AND HONEY SCONES

MAKES
12

PREPARATION TIME: 3 HOURS 30 MINUTES
COOKING TIME: 15 MINUTES

75 g / 2 ½ oz / ⅓ cup butter, cubed

150 g / 5 ½ oz / 1 cup self-raising flour, plus extra for dusting

100 g / 3 ½ oz / ⅔ cup wholemeal flour

150 ml / 5 ½ fl. oz / ⅔ cup milk, plus extra for brushing

4 tbsp runny honey

4 tbsp sesame seeds

METHOD

• Preheat the oven to 220°C (200°C fan) / 425F / gas 7 and line a baking tray with greaseproof paper.

• Rub the butter into the flours with your fingertips until the mixture resembles fine breadcrumbs.

• Pour in the milk and honey and mix together into a pliable dough.

• Turn the dough out onto a floured work surface and press it out into a rectangle, 2 cm thick.

• Use a round pastry cutter to stamp out the scones and transfer them to the baking tray.

• Brush the scones with milk and sprinkle with sesame seeds then bake for 12–15 minutes or until golden brown and cooked through.

• Transfer the scones to a wire rack to cool a little before serving.

SPICED WHOLEMEAL BREAD

MAKES
1

PREPARATION TIME: 2 HOURS 30 MINUTES
COOKING TIME: 35-40 MINUTES

200 g / 7 oz / 1 ⅓ cups strong white bread flour, plus extra for dusting

200 g / 7 oz / 1 ⅓ cups stone-ground wholemeal flour

½ tsp easy blend dried yeast

1 tbsp caster (superfine) sugar

1 tsp fine sea salt

½ tsp ground cloves

½ tsp ground nutmeg

½ tsp ground star anise

½ tsp ground cardamom

½ tsp ground cinnamon

1 tbsp sunflower oil

METHOD

- Mix together the flours, yeast, sugar, salt and spices. Stir the oil into 280 ml of warm water and stir it into the bowl.

- Knead on a lightly oiled surface for 10 minutes or until the dough is smooth and elastic.

- Leave the dough to rest, covered with oiled cling film, for 1-2 hours or until doubled in size.

- Knead the dough for 2 more minutes, then shape it into a loaf.

- Transfer the loaf to a greased baking tray and cover again with oiled clingfilm. Leave to prove for 1 hour or until doubled in size.

- Meanwhile, preheat the oven to 220°C (200°C fan) / 425F / gas 7.

- When the dough has risen, slash the top with a sharp knife.

- Transfer the tray to the top shelf of the oven then quickly throw a small cupful of water onto the floor of the oven and close the door.

- Bake for 35-40 minutes or until the loaf sounds hollow when tapped.

HAZELNUT AND SULTANA BREAD

MAKES
1

PREPARATION TIME: 2 HOURS 30 MINUTES
COOKING TIME: 35–40 MINUTES

200 g / 7 oz / 1 ⅓ cups strong white bread flour, plus extra for dusting

200 g / 7 oz / 1 ⅓ cups stone-ground wholemeal flour

½ tsp easy blend dried yeast

1 tbsp caster (superfine) sugar

1 tsp fine sea salt

100 g / 3 ½ oz hazelnuts (cobnuts), chopped

100 g / 3 ½ oz sultanas

1 tbsp butter, melted

METHOD

• Mix together the flours, yeast, sugar, salt, hazelnuts and sultanas. Stir the butter into 280 ml of warm water.

• Stir the liquid into the dry ingredients then knead on a lightly oiled surface for 10 minutes.

• Leave the dough to rest, covered with oiled cling film, for 1–2 hours or until doubled in size.

• Knead the dough for 2 minutes, then shape into a loaf.

• Transfer the loaf to a greased baking tray and cover again with oiled cling film. Leave to prove for 1 hour.

• Preheat the oven to 220°C (200°C fan) / 425F / gas 7.

• When the dough has risen, slash the top with a knife and dust with flour.

• Transfer the tray to the top shelf of the oven.

• Bake for 35–40 minutes.

OLIVE, MUSHROOM AND HAM LOAF CAKE

SERVES
8

PREPARATION TIME: 10 MINUTES
COOKING TIME: 55 MINUTES

300 g / 10 ½ oz / 2 cups self-raising flour

2 tsp baking powder

250 g / 9 oz / 1 ¼ cups butter, softened

5 large eggs

75 g / 2 ½ oz / ½ cup green olives, pitted and halved

50 g / 1 ¾ oz / ⅔ cup mushrooms, diced

75 g / 2 ½ oz ham, cubed

METHOD

• Preheat the oven to 180°C (160°C fan) / 350F / gas 4 and line a large loaf tin with non-stick baking paper.

• Sieve the flour and baking powder into a mixing bowl and add the butter and eggs.

• Beat the mixture with an electric whisk for 4 minutes or until smooth and well whipped.

• Fold in the olives, mushrooms and ham then scrape the mixture into the loaf tin.

• Bake for 55 minutes or until a skewer inserted comes out clean.

• Transfer the cake to a wire rack and leave to cool completely before serving.

SULTANA BREAD

MAKES
1

PREPARATION TIME: 2 HOURS 30 MINUTES
COOKING TIME: 35 MINUTES

400 g / 14 oz / 2 ⅔ cups strong white bread
flour, plus extra for dusting

½ tsp easy blend dried yeast

1 tbsp caster (superfine) sugar

1 tsp fine sea salt

100 g / 3 ½ oz / ½ cup sultanas

1 tbsp butter, melted

1 egg, beaten

METHOD

- Mix together the flour, yeast, sugar, salt and sultanas. Stir the butter into 280 ml of warm water. Stir the liquid into the dry ingredients then knead on a lightly oiled surface for 10 minutes or until the dough is smooth and elastic.

- Leave the dough to rest, covered with oiled cling film, for 1–2 hours or until doubled in size.

- Knead the dough for 2 minutes, then shape it into a long loaf. Transfer the dough to a greased loaf tin and cover again with oiled cling film. Leave to prove for 1 hour or until doubled in size.

- Meanwhile, preheat the oven to 220°C (200°C fan) / 425F / gas 7.

- When the dough has risen, brush the top with beaten egg and slash a line down the centre. Transfer the tin to the top shelf of the oven. Bake for 35 minutes or until the loaf sounds hollow when tapped.

GRANARY ROLLS

MAKES
8

PREPARATION TIME: 2 HOURS 30 MINUTES
COOKING TIME: 20–25 MINUTES

200 g / 7 oz / 1 ⅓ cups strong white bread flour,
plus extra for dusting

200 g / 7 oz / 1 ⅓ cups malted granary flour

½ tsp easy blend dried yeast

1 tbsp caster (superfine) sugar

1 tsp fine sea salt

3 tbsp sunflower seeds

3 tbsp hemp seeds

1 tbsp sunflower oil

METHOD

- Mix the flours, yeast, sugar, salt and seeds. Stir the oil into 280 ml of warm water and stir it into the bowl.

- Knead on a lightly oiled surface for 10 minutes. Leave the dough to rest, covered with oiled cling film, for 1–2 hours or until doubled in size.

- Knead the dough for 2 more minutes, then shape into 8 large rolls.

- Transfer the rolls to a greased baking tray and cover again with oiled cling film. Prove for 1 hour.

- Preheat the oven to 220°C (200°C fan) / 425F / gas 7.

- When the dough has risen, slash the tops with a sharp knife.

- Transfer the tray to the top shelf of the oven.

- Bake for 20–25 minutes.

RUSTIC BAGUETTES

MAKES
2

PREPARATION TIME: 2 HOURS 30 MINUTES
COOKING TIME: 20–30 MINUTES

350 g / 12 ½ oz / 1 ½ cups strong white bread flour, plus extra for dusting

50 g / 1 ¾ oz / ⅓ cup stone-ground wholemeal flour

½ tsp easy blend dried yeast

1 tbsp caster (superfine) sugar

1 tsp fine sea salt

1 tbsp olive oil

280 ml / 9 ½ fl. oz / 1 cup warm water

METHOD

• Mix the flours, yeast, sugar and salt. Stir the oil into the warm water then stir it into the dry ingredients.

• Knead on a lightly oiled surface for 10 minutes.

• Leave the dough to rest, covered with oiled cling film, for 1–2 hours or until doubled in size.

• Roll the dough into 2 long baguettes and squeeze the ends into a point.

• Transfer the baguettes to a greased baking tray then cover with oiled cling film and leave to prove for 1 hour.

• Preheat the oven to 220°C (200°C fan) / 425F / gas 7.

• Dust the baguettes with a little flour and make diagonal slashes along the top with a sharp knife.

• Transfer the tray to the top shelf of the oven then quickly throw a small cupful of water onto the oven floor and close the door.

• Bake for 20–30 minutes.

WAFFLE BISCUITS

MAKES
36

PREPARATION TIME: 10 MINUTES
COOKING TIME: 1 MINUTE

110 g / 4 oz / ½ cup butter, softened

3 large eggs, beaten

150 g / 5 ½ oz / ⅔ cup caster (superfine) sugar

2 tsp baking powder

225 g / 8 oz / 1 ½ cups self-raising flour

METHOD

- Beat all the ingredients together until smooth.

- Heat a pizzelle iron on the hob until very hot, then add a heaped teaspoon of batter to each waffle indent and close the two halves together.

- Cook the waffles for 30 seconds to 1 minute or until cooked through.

MAINS

SPICY LAMB SAMOSAS

MAKES
6

PREPARATION TIME: 20 MINUTES
COOKING TIME: 35 MINUTES

2 tbsp olive oil

1 small onion, finely chopped

2 cloves of garlic, crushed

250 g / 9 oz / 1 cup minced lamb

¼ tsp chilli (chili) powder

½ tsp ground cumin

½ tsp ground coriander

¼ tsp ground cinnamon

50 g / 1 ¾ oz / ⅓ cup frozen peas, defrosted

225 g / 8 oz filo pastry

100 g / 3 ½ oz / ½ cup butter, melted

METHOD

- Preheat the oven to 180°C (160°C fan) / 350F / gas 4 and grease a large baking tray.

- Heat the oil in a frying pan and fry the onion for 5 minutes or until softened.

- Add the garlic and minced lamb and cook for 5 more minutes then add the spices and peas. Turn off the heat and leave to cool for a few minutes.

- Cut the pile of filo sheets in half then take one halved sheet and brush it with melted butter.

- Arrange a tablespoon of the filling at one end and fold the corner over, then triangle-fold it up.

- Transfer the samosa to the baking tray and repeat with the rest of the filo and filling, then brush with any leftover butter.

- Bake the samosas for 20 minutes, turning half way through, until the pastry is crisp and golden brown.

- Serve with a side of fragrant basmati rice, a wedge of lemon and a sprig of coriander for a light meal.

PEPPER, PANCETTA AND TOMATO FLATBREADS

MAKES
8

PREPARATION TIME: 2 HOURS 30 MINUTES
COOKING TIME: 8–10 MINUTE

400 g / 14 oz / 2 ⅔ cups strong white bread flour, plus extra for dusting

½ tsp easy blend dried yeast

2 tsp caster (superfine) sugar

1 tsp dried herbs de Provence

½ tsp fine sea salt

1 tbsp olive oil

250 g / 9 oz roasted peppers in oil, drained

100 g / 3 ½ oz pancetta, finely chopped

8 cherry tomatoes

8 small sprigs of flowering rosemary

METHOD

- In a large bowl, mix together the flour, yeast, sugar, herbs and salt. Stir the oil into 280 ml of warm water.

- Stir the liquid into the dry ingredients then knead on a lightly oiled surface for 10 minutes or until smooth and elastic.

- Leave the dough to rest covered with oiled cling film for 1–2 hours or until doubled in size.

- Preheat the oven to 220°C (200°C fan) / 425F/ gas 7 and grease 2 large non-stick baking trays.

- Knead the dough for 2 more minutes then divide into 8 pieces.

- Roll each piece of dough into a thin flatbread and transfer to the baking trays.

- Top the flatbreads with the peppers and pancetta and add a cherry tomato and rosemary sprig to each one.

- Transfer the tray to the oven and bake for 8–10 minutes or until each bread is cooked through underneath.

- Serve with a side of roasted peppers, grilled artichokes and olives, for an Italian-inspired light meal.

SALMON GRATIN

SERVES
4

PREPARATION TIME: 10 MINUTES
COOKING TIME: 45 MINUTES

450 g / 1 lb salmon fillet, skinned and cubed

500 ml / 17 ½ fl. oz / 2 cups milk

1 bay leaf

4 tbsp butter

1 leek, chopped

2 tbsp plain flour

3 tbsp breadcrumbs

1 tbsp flat-leaf parsley, finely chopped

12 thin slices chorizo

METHOD

- Preheat the oven to 200°C (180°C fan) / 400F / gas 6.

- Put the milk and bay leaf in a small saucepan and heat until simmering.

- Meanwhile, heat the butter in a small saucepan and fry the leek for 5 minutes.

- Stir in the flour then strain in the milk, stirring constantly. Cook until the sauce is thick and smooth.

- Arrange the salmon in an even layer in a baking dish, then pour over the sauce.

- Sprinkle the sauce with breadcrumbs and parsley and arrange the chorizo on top, then bake for 30 minutes.

LAMB HOTPOT

SERVES
6

PREPARATION TIME: 2 HOURS 30 MINUTES
COOKING TIME: 20–25 MINUTES

900 g / 2 lb boneless lamb neck, cubed

2 lamb kidneys, trimmed and quartered

50 g / 1 ¾ oz / ¼ cup butter

2 tbsp olive oil

2 onions, sliced

a few sprigs of thyme

1 tbsp plain (all-purpose) flour

800 ml / 1 pint 8 oz / 3 ¼ cups lamb stock

900 g / 2 lb potatoes, cut into 3 mm slices

METHOD

- Preheat the oven to 160°C (140°C fan) / 325F / gas 3 and season the lamb liberally with salt and pepper.
- Melt half the butter with the oil in a frying pan over a high heat then sear the lamb and kidneys in batches.
- Remove the meat from the pan, lower the heat and add the onions. Cook for 5 minutes, stirring occasionally.
- Add the garlic and thyme and cook for 2 more minutes.
- Increase the heat and stir in the flour then add the stock.
- Arrange the lamb and kidneys in a casserole dish and pour over the onion liquour.
- Slice the potatoes 3 mm thick with a sharp knife or mandolin and arrange them on top of the lamb.
- Cut the remaining butter into small pieces and dot it over the top of the potatoes then cover the dish tightly with foil or a lid.
- Bake the hotpot for 1 hour 30 minutes then remove the lid and cook for a further hour.

MINI SAUSAGE CASSOULET

MAKES
6

PREPARATION TIME: 10 MINUTES
COOKING TIME: 1 HOUR 45 MINUTES

400 g / 14 oz / 2 ⅔ cups dried haricot beans, soaked overnight

3 litres / 5 pints 6 fl. oz / 12 cups good quality chicken stock

2 tbsp olive oil

6 good quality pork sausages

1 morteau sausage, sliced

100 g / 3 ½ oz chorizo, cubed

2 cloves of garlic, crushed

50 g / 1 ¾ oz / ⅔ cup breadcrumbs

a few sprigs of parsley to garnish

METHOD

• Put the beans in a large saucepan with the stock and simmer gently for 1 hour.

• Meanwhile, heat the oil in a frying pan and brown the sausages all over, then cut them in half.

• Preheat the oven to 150°C (130°C fan) / 300F / gas 2.

• Drain the beans and reserve the stock then stir in the sausages, morteau, chorizo and garlic.

• Divide the mixture between 6 mini casserole dishes, then sprinkle with breadcrumbs.

• Bake the cassoulets for 45 minutes, topping up with extra stock if necessary.

LAMB SHANK AND VEGETABLE TAGINES

MAKES
4

PREPARATION TIME: 5 MINUTES
COOKING TIME: 2 HOURS

lamb shanks

12 baby carrots, peeled

8 spring onions, trimmed

4 small turnips, peeled

6 new potatoes, peeled and halved

400 ml / 14 fl. oz / 1⅔ cups lamb stock

2 cloves of garlic, crushed

1 lemon, juiced

1 tbsp flat-leaf parsley, chopped

METHOD

• Preheat the oven to 180°C (160°C fan) / 350F / gas 4.

• Put each lamb shank in an individual tagine and divide the vegetables between them.

• Mix the lamb stock with the garlic and lemon juice and season well with salt and pepper, then pour it over the lamb and put on the lids.

• Transfer the tagines to the oven and bake for 2 hours.

• Remove the lids and sprinkle with parsley before serving.

TOAD IN THE HOLE

SERVES
4

PREPARATION TIME: 10 MINUTES
COOKING TIME: 1 HOUR 30 MINUTES

1 tbsp lard

75 g / 2 ½ oz / ½ cup plain (all-purpose) flour

2 large eggs

100 ml / 3 ½ oz / ½ cup whole milk

6 good quality pork sausages

salt

METHOD

• Preheat the oven to 230°C (210°C fan) / 450F / gas 8. Put the lard in a baking dish and transfer to the oven to heat.

• Put the flour in a large jug with a pinch of salt and make a well in the centre. Break in the eggs and pour in the milk, then use a whisk to gradually incorporate all of the flour from round the outside.

• Take the baking dish out of the oven and immediately pour in the batter.

• Add the sausages then return the dish to the oven straight away and bake for 30 minutes without opening the oven door.

HADDOCK GRATIN

SERVES
4

PREPARATION TIME: 10 MINUTES
COOKING TIME: 1 HOUR 5 MINUTES

3 large sweet potatoes

50 g / 1 ¾ oz / ¼ cup butter

1 clove of garlic, crushed

500 ml / 17 ½ fl. oz / 2 cups milk

1 bay leaf

400 g / 14 oz smoked haddock fillet

50 g / 1 ¾ oz / ½ cup Red Leicester, grated

1 tbsp chives

METHOD

- Preheat the oven to 200°C (180°C fan) / 400F / gas 6.

- Bake the sweet potatoes in their skins for 45 or until a skewer inserted slides in easily.

- Peel off and discard the skins and mash the flesh with the butter and garlic, seasoning with salt and pepper.

- While the potatoes are cooking, put the milk and bay leaf in a small saucepan and bring to a simmer.

- Lay the haddock in a snugly-fitting dish and pour the hot milk over the top. Cover the dish with cling film and leave to stand for 10 minutes.

- Remove any skin and bones from the haddock then flake the flesh into the mashed sweet potato, adding enough of the milk to make a soft consistency.

- Spoon the mixture into a baking dish and scatter with the cheese and chives then bake for 20 minutes or until the top is golden brown.

TOMATO PASTA BAKE

SERVES
6

PREPARATION TIME: 5 MINUTES
COOKING TIME: 35 MINUTES

a small bunch basil

400 g / 14 oz dried bucatini pasta

2 tbsp olive oil

2 cloves of garlic, crushed

200 g / 7 oz / 1 cup plum tomatoes, chopped

100 g / 3 ½ oz / 1 cup Cheddar cheese, grated

METHOD

• Preheat the oven to 180°C (160°C fan) / 350F / gas 4.

• Strip the basil leaves from the stems and reserve. Cook the bucatini with the basil stems in boiling, salted water according to the package instructions until almost cooked. Drain the pasta well and discard the basil stems.

• Meanwhile, heat the oil in a sauté pan and fry the garlic for 1 minute. Add the tomatoes and cook for 10 minutes, stirring occasionally. Season to taste with salt and pepper.

• When the pasta is ready, stir it into the sauce then tip it into a baking dish and sprinkle with cheese.

• Transfer the dish to the oven and bake for 20 minutes or until the top is golden brown and the pasta has finished cooking. Garnish with the basil leaves just before serving.

BEEF WELLINGTON

SERVES
8

PREPARATION TIME: 5 MINUTES
COOKING TIME: 35 MINUTES

750 g / 1 lb 7 oz beef fillet, in one piece

4 tbsp olive oil

2 tbsp butter

1 large onion, finely chopped

3 cloves of garlic, crushed

2 tbsp fresh thyme leaves

300 g / 10 ½ oz / 4 cups mushrooms, finely chopped

450 g / 1 lb all-butter puff pastry

8 slices prosciutto

1 egg, beaten

sea salt and freshly ground black pepper

METHOD

- Season the beef well with sea salt and black pepper. Heat half of the oil in a large frying pan until smoking hot and then sear the beef on all sides until brown. Leave to cool.

- Add the rest of the oil and the butter to the pan and turn the heat down to medium. Fry the onion for 5 minutes until translucent, then add the garlic and thyme and cook for another minute, stirring all the time. Add the mushrooms and a pinch of salt and cook for 10 minutes or until the liquid that comes out has completely evaporated. Season to taste with salt and pepper, then leave to cool. Blend to a smooth purée in a food processor.

- Preheat the oven to 230°C (210°C fan) / 450F / gas 8. Roll out the pastry on a floured surface into a large rectangle. Spread over the mushroom mixture, and then arrange the prosciutto on top in an even layer.

- Sit the beef on top and enclose in the pastry. Seal the edges and trim away any excess pastry, then brush with beaten egg. Lightly score the top a few times without cutting all the way through the pastry.

- Bake for 35 minutes or until the pastry is golden brown on top and cooked through underneath.

TRADITIONAL STUFFED TOMATOES

SERVES
4

PREPARATION TIME: 10 MINUTES
COOKING TIME: 45 MINUTES

For the tomatoes

6 large vine tomatoes

600 g / 1 lb 5 oz / 4 cups beef mince

30 ml / 1 fl. oz / 2 tbsp sunflower oil

2 cloves of garlic, minced

1 tsp dried oregano

1 tsp dried basil

salt and pepper

TO GARNISH

250 g / 9 oz / 1 1/2 cups cooked white long grain rice

a few sprigs of oregano

METHOD

- Preheat the oven to 190°C (170°C fan) / 375F / gas 5.

- Heat the sunflower oil in a large sauté pan set over a moderate heat.

- Sauté the garlic for 30 seconds before adding the beef mince.

- Cook until browned all over before adding the dried herbs and seasoning to taste.

- Remove to one side to cool as you prepare the tomatoes.

- Remove their tops and reserve to one side before scooping out the seeds and flesh.

- Fill with the beef mince and replace their tops.

- Spoon the rice into an oval baking dish and sprinkle with cold water.

- Sit the stuffed tomatoes on top and bake for 10–12 minutes until warmed through.

- Remove from the oven and garnish with oregano before serving.

VEGETARIAN

BAKED POTATOES WITH SOURED CREAM

MAKES
4

PREPARATION TIME: 2 MINUTES
COOKING TIME: 1 HOUR

4 medium baking potatoes

2 tbsp olive oil

125 g / 4 ½ oz / ½ cup soured cream

2 tbsp chives, chopped

4 bay leaves to garnish

METHOD

- Preheat the oven to 200°C (180°C fan) / 400F / gas 6.

- Rub the potatoes with olive oil and sprinkle with salt then transfer them directly to the top shelf of the oven.

- Bake the potatoes for 1 hour or until a skewer inserted slides in easily.

- While the potatoes are cooking, mix the soured cream with the chives and season to taste with salt and pepper.

- When the potatoes are ready, cut open the tops and spoon in the soured cream, then garnish each one with a bay leaf.

CHEESE PUFFS

MAKES
12

PREPARATION TIME: 15 MINUTES
COOKING TIME: 20 MINUTES

4 tbsp plain (all-purpose) flour

1 egg, beaten

75 g / 2 ½ oz / ½ cup panko breadcrumbs

450 g / 1 lb / 2 cups leftover mashed potato

100 g / 3 ½ oz / 1 cup Cheddar, grated

sunflower oil for deep-frying

basil and sage leaves to serve

METHOD

- Preheat the oven to 230°C (210°C fan) / 450F / gas 8.

- Heat the oil in a frying pan and fry the onion, bacon and garlic for 5 minutes, stirring occasionally.

- Stir in the breadcrumbs, cheese and mustard and season to taste with salt and pepper.

- Roll out the pastry on a lightly floured surface and cut out 12 circles.

- Put a heaped teaspoon of the cheese mixture in the centre of each circle, then fold it in half and seal with beaten egg.

- Crimp the edges, transfer the pastries to a baking tray and brush the tops with egg.

- Bake the puffs for 15 minutes or until golden brown and cooked through.

CAMEMBERT SCONES

MAKES
12

PREPARATION TIME: 10 MINUTES
COOKING TIME: 4–5 MINUTES

4 tbsp plain (all-purpose) flour

1 egg, beaten

75 g / 2 ½ oz / ½ cup panko breadcrumbs

2 camembert, cut into large wedges

sunflower oil for deep-frying

METHOD

- Put the flour, egg and panko breadcrumbs in 3 separate bowls.

- Dip the camembert wedges alternately in the flour, egg and breadcrumbs and shake off any excess.

- Heat the oil in a deep fat fryer, according to the manufacturer's instructions, to a temperature of 180°C.

- Lower the camembert in the fryer basket and cook for 4–5 minutes or until crisp and golden brown.

- Tip the camembert into a kitchen paper lined bowl to remove any excess oil and serve immediately.

RED ONION SAVOURY CHEESECAKE

SERVES
8

PREPARATION TIME: 25 MINUTES
COOKING TIME: 40-30 MINUTES

200 g / 7 oz all-butter puff pastry

3 tbsp olive oil

3 red onions, halved and sliced

450 g / 1 lb / 2 cups cream cheese

100 g / 3 ½ oz soft blue cheese, cubed

50 g / 1 ¾ oz / ½ cup pistachio nuts, chopped

METHOD

- Preheat the oven to 220°C (200°C fan) / 425F / gas 7 and grease a baking tray.

- Roll out the pastry on a lightly floured surface. Invert a large loaf tin on top of the pastry and cut round it, then transfer the pastry to the baking tray and prick with a fork.

- Bake the pastry for 15 minutes or until golden brown and cooked through. Leave to cool.

- Heat the oil in a large sauté pan and fry the onions over a gentle heat for 20 minutes, stirring occasionally.

- Line the loaf tin with cling film then spoon in the onions and level the top.

- Beat the cream cheese with the blue cheese and half of the pistachio nuts and spread it over the onions, then scatter over the rest of the pistachios.

- Put the pastry on top, press down firmly and cover with cling film, then chill in the fridge for 3 hours before unmoulding and slicing.

CHEESE MUFFINS

MAKES
12

PREPARATION TIME: 25 MINUTES
COOKING TIME: 20 MINUTES

100 g / 3 ½ oz / 3 cups fresh spinach

2 large eggs

120 ml / 4 fl. oz / ½ cup sunflower oil

180 ml / 6 fl. oz / ¾ cup Greek yoghurt

110 g / 4 oz / 1 cup Parmesan, grated

175 g / 6 oz / 1 ¾ cups Taleggio, diced

225 g / 8 oz / 1 ½ cups plain (all-purpose) flour

2 tsp baking powder

½ tsp bicarbonate of (baking) soda

½ tsp salt

METHOD

- Preheat the oven to 180°C (160°C fan) / 350F / gas 4 and line a 12-hole muffin tin with paper cases.

- Put the spinach in a large saucepan with 2 tbsp of water. Cover the pan and put over a medium heat for 4 minutes or until the spinach has cooked right down. Squeeze out any excess moisture then chop finely.

- Beat the egg in a jug with the oil and yoghurt then stir in the Parmesan, Taleggio and spinach. Mix the flour, raising agents and salt in a bowl, then pour in the contents of the jug and stir just enough to combine.

- Divide the mixture between the paper cases, then bake in the oven for 20 minutes. Test with a wooden toothpick, if it comes out clean, the muffins are done. Serve warm.

CAMEMBERT STUFFED ONIONS

MAKES
8

PREPARATION TIME: 10 MINUTES
COOKING TIME: 45 MINUTES

8 medium onions, peeled

½ Camembert, cubed

150 g / 5 ½ oz / ¾ cup sun-dried tomatoes in oil,
drained & chopped

2 tbsp oregano leaves

METHOD

- Preheat the oven to 200°C (180°C fan) / 400F / gas 6.

- Simmer the onions in salted water for 10 minutes, then scoop out the centres with a teaspoon and arrange on a baking tray.

- Mix the Camembert with the sun-dried tomatoes and oregano leaves and pack the mixture into the cavities.

- Bake the onions for 35 minutes or until they are tender all the way through.

COUSCOUS AND VEGETABLE GRATIN

SERVES
6

PREPARATION TIME: 30 MINUTES
COOKING TIME: 50 MINUTES

300 g / 10 ½ oz / 1 ¾ cups couscous

2 tbsp olive oil

1 carrot, diced

100 g / 3 ½ oz green (string) beans, chopped

100 g / 3 ½ oz / ⅔ cup podded baby broad beans

2 tbsp pine nuts

2 tbsp flat-leaf parsley, finely chopped

FOR THE TOPPING:

450 g / 1 lb carrots, peeled and chopped

450 g / 1 lb broccoli, broken into florets

100 g / 3 ½ oz / ½ cup butter

50 g / 1 ¾ oz / ½ cup Emmental, grated

METHOD

- Preheat the oven to 200°C (180°C fan) / 400F / gas 6.

- To make the topping, cook the carrots and broccoli in separate pans of salted water for 10 minutes, or until they are tender, then drain well. Add half of the butter to each pan, then blend each one to a puree with an immersion blender.

- Pour 300 ml of boiling water over the couscous then cover and leave to steam for 5 minutes.

- Meanwhile, heat the oil in a frying pan and fry the vegetables and pine nuts for 5 minutes.

- Fluff up the couscous grains with a fork and stir in the vegetables and parsley and transfer the mixture to a baking dish.

- Spread the broccoli puree on top, followed by the carrot puree, then sprinkle with cheese.

- Bake the gratin for 30 minutes or until golden brown.

SQUASH, SPINACH AND RICOTTA LASAGNE

SERVES
4

PREPARATION TIME: 1 HOUR 10 MINUTES
COOKING TIME: 30 MINUTES

1 butternut squash, halved and seeds removed

2 tbsp olive oil

1 onion, finely chopped

2 cloves of garlic, crushed

100 g / 3 ½ oz / 4 cups spinach, washed

250 g / 9 oz / 1 ¼ cups ricotta

¼ tsp nutmeg, freshly grated

300 g / 10 ½ oz fresh lasagne sheets

100 g / 3 ½ oz / 1 cup mozzarella cheese, grated

2 tbsp Parmesan, finely grated

2 tbsp pine nuts

salad leaves, to serve

salt and freshly ground black pepper

METHOD

• Preheat the oven to 190°C (170°C fan) / 375F / gas 5.

• Put the squash, cut side up on a baking tray and cover with foil. Bake in the oven for 50 minutes or until a knife slides easily into the thickest part.

• Meanwhile, heat the oil in a large sauté pan and fry the onion for 10 minutes, stirring occasionally. Add the garlic and stir-fry for 2 minutes.

• Add the spinach to the pan and cover with a lid. Let it wilt in its own steam for 4 minutes, stirring halfway through. Drain off any excess liquid, then season with salt and pepper.

• Season the ricotta with nutmeg, salt and pepper.

• When the squash is ready, scoop the flesh out of the skin into a bowl and mash roughly with a fork. Layer it in a baking dish with the spinach, ricotta and lasagne sheets, finishing with a layer of pasta. Mix the mozzarella with the Parmesan and sprinkle it over the top then scatter over the pine nuts.

• Bake the lasagne for 30 minutes or until piping hot all the way through and bubbling on top. Serve with salad leaves.

RED ONION AND ROSEMARY LOAF CAKE

SERVES
8

PREPARATION TIME: 10 MINUTES
COOKING TIME: 55 MINUTES

3 red onions, sliced

2 tbsp olive oil

300 g / 10 ½ oz / 2 cup self-raising flour

2 tsp baking powder

250 g / 9 oz / 1 ¼ cup butter, softened

5 large eggs

2 tbsp rosemary leaves

METHOD

- Preheat the oven to 170°C (150°C fan) / 340F / gas 3 and line a loaf tin with a paper case.

- Fry the onions in the oil for 10 minutes or until softened and starting to caramelize. Leave to cool.

- Sieve the flour and baking powder into a mixing bowl and add the butter and eggs.

- Beat the mixture with an electric whisk for 4 minutes or until smooth and well whipped.

- Fold in the onions and rosemary then scrape the mixture into the loaf tin.

- Bake for 55 minutes or until a skewer inserted comes out clean.

- Transfer the cake to a wire rack and leave to cool completely before serving.

OLIVE AND ROSEMARY MINI MUFFINS

MAKES
24

PREPARATION TIME: 1 HOUR 10 MINUTES
COOKING TIME: 30 MINUTES

2 large eggs

120 ml / 4 fl. oz / ½ cup sunflower oil

180 ml / 6 fl. oz / ⅔ cup Greek yoghurt

2 tbsp Parmesan, finely grated

225 g / 8 oz / 1 ½ cup plain (all-purpose) flour

2 tsp baking powder

½ tsp bicarbonate of (baking) soda

½ tsp salt

75 g / 2 ½ oz / ½ cup black olives, stoned and chopped

2 tbsp fresh rosemary, chopped

METHOD

• Preheat the oven to 180°C (160°C fan) / 350F / gas 4 and line a 24-hole mini muffin tin with paper cases.

• Beat the egg in a jug with the oil, yoghurt and cheese until well mixed.

• Mix the flour, raising agents, salt, olives and rosemary in a bowl, then pour in the egg mixture and stir just enough to combine.

• Divide the mixture between the paper cases, then bake in the oven for 10–15 minutes.

• Test with a wooden toothpick, if it comes out clean, the muffins are done.

• Serve warm.

DESSERTS

PEACH CRUMBLE

SERVES
4

PREPARATION TIME: 1 HOUR 10 MINUTES
COOKING TIME: 45 MINUTES

16 peaches, peeled, stoned and chopped

125 g / 4 ½ oz / ½ cup butter

150 g / 5 ½ oz / 1 cup plain (all-purpose) flour

40 g / 1 ½ oz / ¼ cup caster (superfine) sugar

METHOD

- Preheat the oven to 180°C (160°C fan) / 350F / gas 4.

- Arrange the peaches in an even layer in a baking dish.

- Rub the butter into the flour and stir in the sugar. Take a handful of the topping and squeeze it into a clump, then crumble it over the fruit. Repeat with the rest of the crumble mixture.

- Bake the crumble for 45 minutes or until the topping is golden and the fruit is bubbling.

CHOCOLATE AND BANANA MERINGUE PIES

MAKES
4

PREPARATION TIME: 55 MINUTES
COOKING TIME: 28 MINUTES

100 g / 3 ½ oz / ½ cup butter, cubed

200 g / 7 oz / 1 ⅓ cups plain
(all-purpose) flour

4 large ripe bananas

1 lime, juiced

75 g / 2 ½ oz / ½ cup dark
chocolate chips

FOR THE MERINGUE:

4 large egg whites

110 g / 4 oz / ½ cup caster
(superfine) sugar

METHOD

- Preheat the oven to 200°C (180°C fan) / 400F / gas 6.

- Rub butter into the flour and add cold water to bind.

- Chill for 30 minutes then roll out on a floured surface.

- Line 4 tart cases with pastry and prick the bases. Line the pastry with cling film and fill with baking beans or rice then bake for 10 minutes.

- Remove the cling film and beans and cook for 8 minutes.

- Mash the bananas with the lime juice until smooth then stir in half of the chocolate chips. Divide the mixture between the pastry cases.

- Whisk the egg whites until stiff, then gradually add the sugar and whisk until the mixture is thick and shiny.

- Spoon into a piping bag and pipe onto the tarts. Return the tarts to the oven to bake for 10 minutes.

- Sprinkle over the remaining chocolate chips and serve.

RASPBERRY UPSIDE-DOWN CAKE

SERVES
6

PREPARATION TIME: 15 MINUTES
COOKING TIME: 20 MINUTES

1100 g / 3 ½ oz / ⅔ cup self-raising flour

1 tsp baking powder

100 g / 3 ½ oz / ½ cup caster (superfine) sugar

100 g / 3 ½ oz / ½ cup butter, softened

2 large eggs

250 g / 9 oz / 2 cups fresh raspberries

icing (confectioners') sugar for dusting

METHOD

- Preheat the oven to 180°C (160°C fan) / 350F / gas 4 and butter a 20 cm round cake tin.

- Sieve the flour and baking powder into a mixing bowl and add sugar, butter and eggs.

- Beat the mixture with an electric whisk for 4 minutes or until smooth and well whipped.

- Arrange half of the raspberries in the cake tin and spoon the cake mixture on top.

- Level the cake mixture with a palette knife and bake for 25 minutes or until a skewer inserted comes out clean.

- Leave the cake to cool for 20 minutes before turning out onto a serving plate.

- Top with the rest of the raspberries and sprinkle with icing sugar just before serving.

MINI PEAR QUINOA CRUMBLES

MAKES
4

PREPARATION TIME: 15 MINUTES
COOKING TIME: 40 MINUTES

1200 g / 7 oz / 1 cup quinoa

1 cinnamon stick

4 pears, peeled and cubed

2 tbsp caster (superfine) sugar

50 g / 1 ¾ oz / ¼ cup butter, melted

50 g / 1 ¾ oz / ½ cup ground almonds

75 g / 2 ½ oz / ½ cup dark brown sugar

METHOD

• Preheat the oven to 200°C (180°C fan) / 400F / gas 6.

• Put the quinoa and cinnamon in a saucepan with 450 ml water and bring to the boil. Cover the pan, then reduce the heat and simmer gently for 15 minutes or until all the water has been absorbed.

• Spread the quinoa out onto a tray and leave to steam dry for a few minutes.

• Toss the pears with the caster sugar and divide them between 4 individual baking dishes.

• Stir the melted butter, ground almonds and brown sugar into the quinoa, then sprinkle the mixture on top of the pears.

• Bake the crumbles in the oven for 25 minutes or until the tops are golden brown.

PRUNE CLAFOUTIS

SERVES
6

PREPARATION TIME: 10 MINUTES
COOKING TIME: 35–45 MINUTES

75 g / 2 ½ oz ⅓ cup caster (superfine) sugar

75 g / 2 ½ oz ⅓ cup butter

300 ml / 10 ½ fl. oz / 1 ¼ cups whole milk

2 large eggs

50 g / 1 ¾ oz ⅓ cup plain (all-purpose) flour

2 tbsp ground almonds

300 g / 10 ½ oz / 2 cups stoneless prunes

freshly grated nutmeg for sprinkling

METHOD

- Preheat the oven to 190°C (170°C fan) / 375F / gas 5.

- Melt the butter in a saucepan and cook over a low heat until it starts to smell nutty.

- Brush a little of the butter around the inside of a baking dish then add a spoonful of caster sugar and shake to coat.

- Whisk together the milk and eggs with the rest of the butter.

- Sift the flour into a mixing bowl with a pinch of salt, then stir in the ground almonds and the rest of the sugar.

- Make a well in the middle of the dry ingredients and gradually whisk in the liquid, incorporating all the flour from round the outside until you have a lump-free batter.

- Arrange the prunes in the prepared baking dish, pour over the batter and grate over a little nutmeg.

- Bake the clafoutis for 35–45 minutes or until a skewer inserted in the centre comes out clean.

FOREST FRUIT CRUMBLE

SERVES
6

PREPARATION TIME: 10 MINUTES
COOKING TIME: 50 MINUTES

450 g / 1 lb / 3 cups mixed forest fruits
(defrosted if frozen)

4 tbsp caster (superfine) sugar

75 g / 2 ½ oz ⅓ cup butter

50 g / 1 ¾ oz / ⅓ cup plain (all-purpose) flour

25 g / 1 oz / ¼ cup ground almonds

40 g / 1 ½ oz / ¼ cup light
brown sugar

METHOD

• Preheat the oven to 180°C (160°C fan) / 350F / gas 4.

• Mix the forest fruits with the sugar and arrange in an even layer in the bottom of a baking dish.

• Rub the butter into the flour and stir in the ground almonds and brown sugar.

• Squeeze a handful of the mixture into a clump and then crumble it over the fruit. Use up the rest of the topping in the same way, then shake the dish to level the top.

• Bake the crumble for 40 minutes or until the topping is golden brown and the fruit is bubbling.

MINI CHERRY CLAFOUTIS

SERVES
8

PREPARATION TIME: 10 MINUTES
COOKING TIME: 45 MINUTES

75 g / 2 ½ oz / ⅓ cup caster (superfine) sugar

75 g / 2 ½ oz / ⅓ cup butter

300 ml / 10 ½ fl. oz / 1 ¼ cups
whole milk

2 large eggs

50 g / 1 ¾ oz / ⅓ cup plain (all-purpose) flour

2 tbsp ground almonds

300 g / 10 ½ oz / 2 cups cherries, stoned

4 tbsp flaked (slivered) almonds

icing (confectioners') sugar
for dusting

METHOD

- Preheat the oven to 190°C (170°C fan) / 375F / gas 5.

- Melt the butter in a saucepan and cook over a low heat until it starts to smell nutty.

- Brush a little of the butter around the inside of 8 ramekins then sprinkle with caster sugar and shake to coat.

- Whisk together the milk and eggs with the rest of the butter.

- Sift the flour into a mixing bowl with a pinch of salt, then stir in the ground almonds and the rest of the sugar.

- Make a well in the middle of the dry ingredients and gradually whisk in the liquid, incorporating all the flour from round the outside until you have a lump-free batter.

- Arrange the prunes in the prepared ramekins, then pour in the batter and scatter with flaked almonds.

- Bake the clafoutis for 15–20 minutes or until a skewer inserted in the centre comes out clean.

TWO-FRUIT CRUMBLE

SERVES
6

PREPARATION TIME: 15 MINUTES
COOKING TIME: 25 MINUTES

42 apples, peeled, cored and diced

150 g / 5 ½ oz / 1 cup blackcurrants

4 tbsp caster (superfine) sugar

75 g / 2 ½ oz / ⅓ cup butter, chilled and cubed

75 g / 2 ½ oz / ½ cup plain (all-purpose) flour

25 g / 1 oz / ¼ cup ground almonds

40 g / 1 ½ oz / ¼ cup light brown sugar

2 tbsp flaked (slivered) almonds

METHOD

• Preheat the oven to 180°C (160°C fan) / 350F / gas 4.

• Toss the apples and blackcurrants with the caster sugar and divide between six ramekin dishes.

• Rub the butter into the flour and stir in the ground almonds, brown sugar and flaked almonds. Sprinkle the mixture over the fruit, then bake for 25 minutes or until the tops are golden brown.

CHOC AND PEAR CRUMBLE

SERVES
6

PREPARATION TIME: 10 MINUTES
COOKING TIME: 25 MINUTES

225 g / 8 oz / 1 ⅓ cups light brown sugar

100 g / 3 ½ oz / ½ cup caster (superfine) sugar

2 tbsp runny honey

175 g / 6 oz / ¾ cup butter, melted

1 large egg, plus 1 egg yolk

250 g / 9 oz / 1 ⅔ cups self-raising flour

100 g / 3 ½ oz / 1 cup porridge oats

100 g / 3 ½ oz / ⅔ cup dark chocolate chunks

4 large ripe pears, peeled, cored and diced

METHOD

- Preheat the oven to 160°C (140°C fan) / 325F / gas 3.

- Cream together the two sugars, honey and butter until pale and well-whipped, then beat in the egg and yolk, followed by the flour, oats and chocolate chips.

- Arrange the diced pear in a baking dish, then top with the crumble mixture.

- Bake for 25 minutes or until a skewer inserted in the centre comes out clean. Serve warm.

LITTLE APPLE CRUMBLES

MAKES
4

PREPARATION TIME: 10 MINUTES
COOKING TIME: 30 MINUTES

2 cooking apples, peeled, cored and diced

4 tbsp caster (superfine) sugar

75 g / 2 ½ oz / ⅓ cup butter

50 g / 1 ¾ oz / ⅓ cup plain (all-purpose) flour

25 g / 1 oz / ¼ cup ground almonds

40 g / 1 ½ oz / ¼ cup light brown sugar

METHOD

- Preheat the oven to 180°C (160°C fan) / 350F / gas 4.

- Put the apples in a saucepan with the sugar and a splash of water and cook with the lid on for 5 minutes or until softened.

- Meanwhile, rub the butter into the flour and stir in the ground almonds and brown sugar.

- Divide the cooked apple between 4 small baking dishes.

- Squeeze a handful of the crumble mixture into a clump and then crumble it over the apples. Use up the rest of the topping in the same way, then shake the dishes to level the tops.

- Bake the crumbles for 25 minutes or until the tops are golden brown.

BREAD AND BUTTER PUDDING

SERVES
4

PREPARATION TIME: 35 MINUTES
COOKING TIME: 40 MINUTES

1 loaf white bread, cut into thick slices

3 tbsp butter, softened

200 g / 7 oz / ¾ cup fig jam

250 ml / 9 fl. oz / 1 cup whole milk

200 ml / 7 fl. oz / ¾ cup double (heavy) cream

4 large egg yolks

75 g / 2 ½ oz / ⅓ cup caster (superfine) sugar

METHOD

- Spread the bread with butter and cut it into triangles.

- Arrange the triangles in a baking dish, adding spoonfuls of the jam as you go.

- Whisk the milk, cream, eggs and caster sugar together and pour it over the top, then leave to soak for 30 minutes.

- Preheat the oven to 180°C (160°C fan) / 350F / gas 4.

- Bake the pudding for 40 minutes or until the top is golden brown.

APPLE CHARLOTTE WITH TOFFEE SAUCE

SERVES
6

PREPARATION TIME: 15 MINUTES
COOKING TIME: 40 MINUTES

3 bramley apples, peeled, cored and cubed

100 g / 3 ½ oz / ½ cup brown sugar

½ tsp mixed spice

1 lemon, zest finely grated

1 loaf white bread, sliced and crusts removed

75 g / 2 ½ oz / ⅓ cup butter, softened

FOR THE TOFFEE SAUCE:

100 g / 3 ½ oz / ½ cup butter

100 g / 3 ½ oz / ½ cup muscovado sugar

100 g / 3 ½ oz / ⅓ cup golden syrup

100 ml / 3 ½ fl. oz / ½ cup double (heavy) cream

METHOD

- First make the toffee sauce. Put all of the sauce ingredients in a small saucepan and stir over a low heat until the sugar dissolves.

- Bring to the boil then take off the heat and leave to cool to room temperature. Chill the sauce for 1 hour to thicken.

- Preheat the oven to 180°C (160°C fan) / 350F / gas 4.

- Mix the apples with the sugar, spice and lemon zest in a saucepan then cook, covered, over a medium heat for 8 minutes, stirring occasionally.

- Butter the bread and cut each slice into quarters.

- Line a deep 20 cm round spring-form cake tin with some of the bread and fill with half of the apple.

- Top with more bread slices and spoon in the rest of the apple before adding a final layer of bread.

- Bake the charlotte for 30 minutes or until the top is golden brown. Unmould the cake and cut into wedges, then spoon over the chilled toffee sauce.

MINI PEAR AND HAZELNUT TATIN

MAKES
4

PREPARATION TIME: 10 MINUTES
COOKING TIME: 40 MINUTES

3 tbsp butter, softened and cubed

4 small pears, peeled, halved and cored

4 tbsp soft light brown sugar

100 ml / 3 ½ fl. oz / ½ cup apple juice

100 g / 3 ½ oz / ½ cup hazelnuts
(cobnuts)

300 g / 10 ½ oz all-butter puff pastry

METHOD

- Preheat the oven to 220°C (200°C fan) / 425F / gas 7.

- Melt the butter in a frying pan then fry the pears, cut side down in a single layer, for 5 minutes or until they start to colour.

- Stir the sugar into the apple juice, pour it over the pears then cook until the liquid has reduced to a syrupy glaze.

- Arrange 2 pears in each hole of a 4-hole Yorkshire pudding tin, then stir the hazelnuts into the glaze and spoon them over and around the pears.

- Roll out the pastry on a floured surface and cut out 4 circles the same diameter as the holes.

- Lay the pastry over the pears and tuck in the edges, then transfer the tin to the oven and bake for 25 minutes or until the pastry is golden brown and cooked through.

- Using oven gloves, put a large plate or chopping board on top of the tin and turn them both over in one smooth movement to unmould the tarts.

SPICED PINEAPPLE AND LIME CRUMBLES

MAKES
6

PREPARATION TIME: 10 MINUTES
COOKING TIME: 25 MINUTES

150 ml / 5 ½ fl. oz / ⅔ cup pineapple juice

1 lime, juiced and zest thinly pared

1 cinnamon stick, halved

1 vanilla pod, split lengthways

1 pineapple, peeled, cored and cubed

75 g / 2 ½ oz / ⅓ cup butter

50 g / 1 ¾ oz / ⅓ cup plain (all-purpose) flour

25 g / 1 oz / ¼ cup ground almonds

40 g / 1 ½ oz / ¼ cup caster (superfine) sugar

METHOD

- First make the toffee sauce. Put all of the sauce ingredients in a small saucepan and stir Preheat the oven to 180°C (160°C fan) / 350F / gas 4.

- Put the pineapple juice and lime juice in a small saucepan with the cinnamon and vanilla and simmer for 5 minutes or until syrupy.

- Divide the pineapple between 6 disposable baking dishes and spoon over the spiced pineapple juice, discarding the spices.

- Rub the butter into the flour and stir in the ground almonds, sugar and lime zest.

- Take a handful of the topping and squeeze it into a clump, then crumble it over the fruit.

- Repeat with the rest of the crumble mixture then bake for 25 minutes or until the topping is golden brown.

CHOCOLATE BROWNIES

MAKES
9

PREPARATION TIME: 25 MINUTES
COOKING TIME: 15–20 MINUTES

110 g / 4 oz milk chocolate, chopped

85 g / 3 oz / ¾ cup unsweetened
cocoa powder, sifted

225 g / 8 oz / 1 cup butter

450 g /15 oz / 2 ½ cups light brown sugar

4 large eggs

110 g / 4 oz / ⅔ cup self-raising flour

METHOD

- Preheat the oven to 170°C (150°C fan) / 340F / gas 3 and oil and line a 20 cm x 20 cm (8 in x 8 in) square cake tin.

- Melt the chocolate, cocoa and butter together in a saucepan, then leave to cool a little.

- Whisk the sugar and eggs together with an electric whisk for 3 minutes or until very light and creamy.

- Pour in the chocolate mixture and sieve over the flour, then fold everything together until evenly mixed.

- Scrape into the tin and bake for 35–40 minutes or until the outside is set, but the centre is still quite soft, as it will continue to cook as it cools.

- Leave the brownie to cool completely before cutting into 9 squares.

PISTACHIO BROWNIES

MAKES
8

PREPARATION TIME: 24 MINUTES
COOKING TIME: 15-20 MINUTES

10 g / 4 oz milk chocolate, chopped

85 g / 3 oz / ¾ cup unsweetened cocoa powder, sifted

225 g / 8 oz / 1 cup butter

450 g / 1 lb / 2 ½ cups light brown sugar

4 large eggs

110 g / 4 oz / 1 cup self-raising flour

75 g / 2 ½ oz / ½ cup pistachio nuts, chopped

75 g / 2 ½ oz / ½ cup walnuts, chopped

icing (confectioners') sugar for dusting

METHOD

- Preheat the oven to 160°C (140°C fan) / 325F / gas 3 and oil and line a 20 cm x 20 cm / (8 in x 8 in) square cake tin.

- Melt the chocolate, cocoa and butter together in a saucepan, then leave to cool a little.

- Whisk the sugar and eggs together with an electric whisk for 3 minutes or until very light and creamy.

- Pour in the chocolate mixture and sieve over the flour, then fold everything together with the nuts until evenly mixed.

- Scrape into the tin and bake for 35–40 minutes or until the outside is set, but the centre is still quite soft.

- Leave the brownie to cool completely before cutting into 8 rectangles and dusting with icing sugar.

CHOCO-NUT COOKIES

MAKES
12

PREPARATION TIME: 10 MINUTES
COOKING TIME: 12–15 MINUTES

175 g / 6 oz / ¾ cup butter, melted

225 g / 8 oz / 1 ⅔ cups dark
brown sugar

100 g / 3 ½ oz / ½ cup caster
(superfine) sugar

2 tsp vanilla extract

1 egg, plus 1 egg yolk

250 g / 9 oz / 1 ⅔ cups self-raising flour

175 g / 6 oz / 1 ¼ cups chocolate chips

175 g / 6 oz / 1 ½ cups hazelnuts (cobnuts),
chopped

METHOD

- Preheat the oven to 170°C (150°C fan) / 340F / gas 3 and line 2 baking sheets with greaseproof paper.

- Cream together the two sugars, butter and vanilla extract until pale and well whipped then beat in the egg and yolk, followed by the flour, chocolate and hazelnuts.

- Drop tablespoons of the mixture onto the prepared trays, leaving plenty of room to spread.

- Bake the cookies in batches for 12–15 minutes or until the edges are starting to brown, but the centres are still chewy.

- Transfer to a wire rack and leave to cool.

INDEX